D1442256

The Library of
HOLIDAYS™

CONTRA COSTA COUNTY LIBRARY

CHINESE NEW YEAR

LESLIE C. KAPLAN

The Rosen Publishing Group's
PowerKids Press™

To Marika

Published in 2004 by The Rosen Publishing Group, Inc.
29 East 21st Street, New York, NY 10010

First Edition

Editor: Jannell Khu

Book Design: Michael de Guzman and Michael J. Caroleo

Photo Credits: Cover © Robert Holmes/CORBIS; p. 4 © CORBIS; p. 7 © Paul Almasy/CORBIS; p. 8 © Michael S. Yamashita/CORBIS; p. 11 © Jack Fields/CORBIS; pp. 12, 15, 16 © Phil Schermeister/CORBIS; p. 19 © Keren Su/CORBIS; pp. 20, 22 © Kevin Fleming/CORBIS.

Kaplan, Leslie C.
Chinese New Year / Leslie C. Kaplan.
    p. cm. — (The library of holidays)
Includes bibliographical references and index.
ISBN 0-8239-6658-5
1. New Year—China—Juvenile literature. 2. Chinese Americans—Social life and customs—Juvenile literature. [1. Chinese New Year. 2. Holidays.] I. Title. II. Series.
  GT4905 .K38 2004
  394.261—dc21

                                                                    2002006972

Manufactured in the United States of America

CONTENTS

CHINESE NEW YEAR

The most important Chinese holiday is the celebration of the new year. This is a time when families and friends gather for feasts, fireworks, and parades. Chinese New Year is also a time to honor **ancestors**.

The first day of Chinese New Year usually falls in January or February. The holiday lasts for 15 days. Many people celebrate only the eve, the first few days, and the last day of Chinese New Year. Those people who are **traditional** observe the entire holiday.

For centuries the Chinese have ended the New Year holiday with a dragon parade, as shown in this picture.

THE LUNAR NEW YEAR

The first day of Chinese New Year starts on the first day of the **lunar** year. This date is determined by the lunar calendar, which uses the Moon and its **cycles** to keep track of time. The lunar year arrives in January or February. Years and months of the lunar calendar are represented by 12 animals. Many **Asians** use the lunar calendar and celebrate the lunar new year. The Vietnamese call it *tet nguyen dan,* or "first morning of the first day of the new year." Koreans call the new year *jung whur,* or "first month of the new year."

The rabbit on top of this piece of art shows that the art was made for the year of the rabbit. ▶

A MONSTER CALLED NIEN

The **origins** of the Chinese New Year celebration are told in ancient Chinese **legends**. One story says that a monster named Nien used to eat people on New Year's Eve. After two years of this, the villagers lit loud firecrackers and pasted red banners on their doors to scare Nien. It worked! Nien fled from the noise and the red banners, which looked like flames. To celebrate, the villagers danced, feasted, and exchanged gifts. Today's Chinese New Year holiday includes these practices.

The legend says that Nien was frightened by the loud noise of exploding firecrackers.

NEW YEAR PREPARATIONS

Holiday preparations begin weeks before the new year arrives. The Chinese clean their homes from top to bottom. They do this to sweep away bad luck and to prepare their houses for good luck. Homes are decorated with flowers, such as the plum blossom. This flower stands for **longevity** and wealth. Families spend much time shopping for and cooking the delicious foods that will be eaten throughout the holiday. They put away knives after using them to prevent them from cutting away good luck in the new year.

During the Chinese New Year, homes are decorated with signs that say "good luck," as shown here. ▶

CHINESE NEW YEAR'S EVE

Chinese New Year's Eve is called *ch'u hsi*. On this day, people go to temple to pray for their ancestors. They also pray for health, happiness, and good fortune. Foods eaten on ch'u hsi have special meaning. Chicken and fish are served whole to represent completeness. Noodle strands **symbolize** long life! A Chinese saying states that the longer children stay up on this night, the longer their parents will live. At midnight, fireworks light up the sky.

Chinese New Year dishes may include roasted chicken that is served whole, seafood platters, and soup served inside a carved melon bowl.

GOOD LUCK MONEY

On New Year's Eve, boys and girls receive money stuffed inside *lai-sees*, or small red envelopes. For the rest of the holiday, children and young unmarried adults also receive lai-see gifts from older relatives. These gifts are meant to bring good luck to the entire family. Coins are considered bad luck, so people only give gifts of paper money. Lai-sees come decorated with gold Chinese characters. The characters for fortune, good luck, happiness, and **prosperity** are used often.

During Chinese New Year, children receive red envelopes filled with money! ▶

NEW YEAR'S DAY

Visiting begins on the first day of Chinese New Year. People say "*Gung hay fat choy!*" in greeting. This means "May you prosper!" Guests bring gifts of fruit, sweets, and plants. The gifts have special meaning. Candied coconut represents togetherness. **Lotus seeds** are given to newlyweds so that they will be blessed with many children. People are on their best behavior on New Year's Day. It is thought that what happens on this day decides one's fortune for the entire year.

◀ *People give gifts of oranges throughout Chinese New Year. The oranges are a symbol of wealth and joy.*

THE LION DANCE

Two weeks of celebration follow the first day of Chinese New Year. During the third fourth, and fifth days, some people wear lion costumes and dance along the streets of Chinese neighborhoods throughout the world. According to legend, lion dances scare away evil spirits. Musicians play **gongs** and drums as the lions dance. The lion dancers visit stores to bring the shopkeepers good luck. In turn, the dancers collect money from the shopkeepers. The money is given to the poor.

In the past, people believed that lion dances scared away evil spirits. ▶

THE DRAGON PARADE

On the fifteenth day of Chinese New Year, the holiday ends with a big dragon parade. People carry colorful **lanterns** in the parade. **Acrobats** and musicians perform. A colorful dragon made of wood, silk, and paper appears as firecrackers explode. The dragon is a **mythical** animal that symbolizes strength and goodness in Chinese legends. The dragon chases a large pearl, which stands for wealth. The dragon and its pearl chase stand for wishes of good fortune for the new year.

◄ *Several people are needed to carry the large dragon. The dragon chases the fiery pearl.*

NEW TRADITIONS

New traditions add to the fun of Chinese New Year celebrations. Since 1953, San Francisco's Chinatown has held a Chinese New Year parade. Lion dancers and a 200-foot-long (61-m-long) dragon are just part of the parade. There are also marching bands and parade floats. New York City began a tradition in 2000. The Empire State Building lights up in red and gold during Chinese New Year. However communities celebrate the holiday, it remains a happy time when people gather to welcome the new year.

GLOSSARY

acrobats (A-kruh-bats) Those who have good control of their bodies and can tumble, leap, flip over, and quickly change positions.

ancestors (AN-ses-turz) Relatives who lived long ago.

Asians (AY-zhinz) People who are from the continent called Asia.

cycles (SY-kulz) Series of events that are repeated in the same order.

gongs (GONGZ) Disks of metal that make a ringing sound when they are hit with a hammer.

lanterns (LAN-ternz) Movable lamps with coverings of paper or glass.

legends (LEH-jendz) Stories passed down that many people believe.

longevity (lahn-JEH-vih-tee) A long life span.

lotus seeds (LOH-tus SEEDZ) Seeds from a kind of water plant.

lunar (LOO-ner) Of or about the Moon.

mythical (MITH-ih-kul) Based on or described in a legend; not real.

origins (OR-ih-jinz) The sources from where things began.

prosperity (prah-SPEHR-ih-tee) Success.

symbolize (SIM-buh-lyz) To stand for something important.

traditional (truh-DIH-shuh-nul) Used to doing things in a way that has been passed down over time.

INDEX

WEB SITES

Due to the changing nature of Internet links, PowerKids Press has developed an online list of Web sites related to the subject of this book. This site is updated regularly. Please use this link to access the list:
www.powerkidslinks.com/LHOL/chinese/